Table of Contents

Dedication *1*

Chapter 1: Understanding the Importance of Financial Literacy

What Is Financial Literacy 2

Why It Matters for Today's Teens 4

The Long-Term Benefits of Being Financially Savvy 6

Chapter 2: Budgeting Basics for Young Adults

The Purpose of a Budget 8

How to Create Your First Budget 10

Tracking Income and Expenses 11

Adjusting Your Budget Over Time 13

Chapter 3: Navigating Money Management Apps for Teens

Overview of Popular Financial Apps *16*

Features to Look For in Money Management Apps 18

How to Use Apps Effectively for Budgeting 20

Security and Privacy Considerations 22

Chapter 4: The Importance of Setting Financial Goals

Understanding Short-Term vs Long-Term Goals 24

How to Set Realistic and Achievable Goals...26

The Role of Saving and Achieving Goals...28

Celebrating Milestones...30

Chapter 5: Building a Positive Money Mindset

Understanding Your Attitude Towards Money...32

Overcoming Common Financial Fears...34

Developing Healthy Financial Habits...35

The Power of Gratitude and Generosity...37

Chapter 6: Involving Parents in Financial Learning

The Role of Parents in Financial Education...40

Open Conversations About Money...42

Family Activities to Promote Financial Literacy...44

Encouraging Joint Goal Setting...45

Chapter 7: Real-Life Applications of Financial Literacy

Case Studies of Successful Young Savers...48

Practical Exercises for Parents and Teens...50

Resources for Continued Learning...51

The Journey Ahead: Lifelong Financial Literacy...53

BONUS: Monthly Budget Planner...56

Dedication:

To Frederick L. Harris, Jr. my beloved father and first teacher.

A man who exemplified immense strength, resilience and provided a haven of love, dedication and never-ending support. Always guiding my path, showing me the importance of education while making me feel I could accomplish anything.

This book is a testament to his memory and enduring spirit.

Chapter 1: Understanding the Importance of Financial Literacy

What is Financial Literacy?

Financial literacy is the ability to understand and effectively manage personal finances. It encompasses a variety of skills and knowledge, including budgeting, saving, investing, and understanding credit. For teenagers, gaining financial literacy is extremely crucial as it lays the foundation for responsible money management in adulthood. This understanding can empower young people to navigate their financial futures with confidence and make informed decisions that will benefit them in the long run.

One of the key components of financial literacy is budgeting. Learning how to create and stick to a budget helps teenagers gain insight into their spending habits and prioritize their financial goals. By using budgeting basics, they can track their income and expenses, ensuring they live within their means. This practice not only fosters discipline but also encourages young adults to save for future needs, whether it's for college, a car, or other significant purchases.

Another important aspect is understanding money management apps, which can be particularly appealing to tech-savvy teens. These apps provide a user-friendly way to monitor finances, make budgets, and even learn about investing. By incorporating technology into their financial education, teenagers can engage with their finances in a more interactive manner. This approach not only makes learning about money management enjoyable but also instills a sense of responsibility as they become more accountable for their financial decisions.

Setting financial goals is also a vital part of developing financial literacy. Teens should be encouraged to set short-term and long-term goals, such as saving for a new gadget or planning for college expenses. With guidance and having clear objectives, they can better understand the importance of saving and budgeting. This goal-oriented mindset can motivate them to make smarter financial choices and work towards achieving their aspirations, fostering a sense of accomplishment along the way.

Lastly, building a positive money mindset from a young age can significantly impact a teenager's financial journey. Encouraging a healthy relationship with money, where it is viewed as a tool rather than a source of stress, can lead to more responsible financial behaviors. Parents play a crucial role in modeling these attitudes, helping their children develop confidence in managing their finances. Overall, financial literacy is not just about understanding money, it is also about cultivating skills and attitudes that will serve teens well throughout their lives.

Why It Matters for Today's Teens

In today's fast-paced world, financial literacy has become an essential skill for everyone. Understanding the basics of budgeting can empower young adults to take control of their finances from an early age. By learning to manage their money wisely, teens can develop habits that will serve them well into adulthood, ultimately leading to greater financial stability and independence. This knowledge is not just about managing expenses but about making informed decisions that will impact their future.

With modern technology, money management apps are increasingly popular among teenagers, providing them with accessible tools to track their spending and savings in real time. These apps can simplify complex financial concepts, making it easier for young people to learn as they go. By engaging with these digital resources, teenagers can gain hands-on experience in monitoring their financial behaviors, which is extremely crucial in fostering a responsible attitude towards money.

Setting financial goals is another vital aspect of financial literacy. When teenagers learn to set realistic and achievable financial objectives, they cultivate a sense of purpose and motivation in their financial journey. This practice not only helps them save for desired items, such as a new phone or a car, but also instills a sense of accomplishment when they reach their milestones. Understanding the importance of goalsetting can shape their financial mindset for the better.

Building a positive money mindset from a young age can significantly influence a teenager's relationship with money. Encouraging them to view it as a tool for achieving their dreams rather than a source of stress is crucial. By fostering a healthy attitude towards finances, parents and educators can help teenagers develop the resilience and confidence needed in making financial decisions, paving the way for a prosperous future.

Ultimately, the importance of financial literacy for today's teenagers cannot be overstated. As they transition into adulthood, the skills they acquire in budgeting, goal setting, and money management will be invaluable. It is essential that parents and educators work together to provide teenagers with the knowledge and resources they need to navigate their financial futures successfully. Investing in their financial education today will yield positive results for generations to come.

The Long-Term Benefits of Being Financially Savvy

Being financially savvy is not just about managing money, it's about establishing a foundation for a secure future. When teenagers learn to budget effectively, they develop crucial skills that will serve them throughout their lives. Understanding the principles of budgeting helps them make informed decisions, prioritize their spending, and avoid unnecessary debt. This knowledge empowers them to take control of their financial destinies from a young age.

Moreover, financial literacy goes beyond mere budgeting, it encompasses a wide array of skills, including the effective use of money management apps. These tools can simplify tracking expenses and setting savings goals. By becoming proficient in using such apps, teenagers can gain a clearer picture of their finances, leading to better planning and increased savings. The ability to monitor their financial health in real-time fosters responsible behaviors that can last a lifetime.

Setting financial goals is another essential aspect of being financially savvy. When teenagers understand the importance of goal setting, they learn to envision their future and work towards it systematically. This also makes them more aware of their spending. Whether saving for a new gadget or planning for higher education, having clear objectives instills a sense of purpose in their financial activities. This practice encourages discipline, patience, and a proactive approach to money management.

Building a positive money mindset from a young age can lead to lifelong benefits. When teenagers develop a healthy relationship with money, they are less likely to fall into the traps of impulsive spending or financial anxiety. Instead, they cultivate confidence in their financial decisions, fostering resilience in the face of economic challenges. This mindset is crucial, as it influences their financial behavior well into adulthood, impacting their overall quality of life.

Ultimately, the long-term benefits of being financially savvy are profound. Parents play a vital role in guiding their teenagers towards understanding financial concepts and making wise decisions. By nurturing these skills, families can pave the way for future financial independence and security. The lessons learned today will not only empower teenagers but also help create a financially literate generation that values responsible money management.

Chapter 2: Budgeting Basics for Young Adults

The Purpose of a Budget

A budget serves as a fundamental tool for both parents and teenagers, guiding them in their financial journey. It acts as a roadmap, helping young adults understand where their money comes from and where it goes. By creating a budget, teenagers can learn to allocate their resources wisely, ensuring that they can save for future goals while managing their day-to-day expenses. This foundational skill not only empowers them to make informed decisions but also fosters a sense of responsibility towards their finances.

One of the primary purposes of a budget is to facilitate financial literacy among teenagers. As they learn to track their income and expenditures, they gain valuable insights into money management. This knowledge equips them with the ability to distinguish between wants and needs, which is extremely important and an essential skill in today's consumer-driven society. By recognizing the importance of prioritizing their spending, teenagers can avoid unnecessary debt and build a solid financial future.

In this digital age, understanding budgeting apps can greatly enhance a teenager's ability to manage their finances. These tools provide an interactive way to track spending, set financial goals, and even save money. Parents can encourage their teens to explore various money management apps that are designed specifically for young adults, making the budgeting process engaging and effective. By leveraging technology, teenagers can embrace budgeting as a lifestyle rather than a chore.

Setting financial goals is another crucial aspect of budgeting. It helps teenagers envision their future and work towards achieving their dreams, whether it's saving for a new gadget or planning for college. A budget acts as a practical guide for these goals, allowing young adults to break down their aspirations into manageable steps. This practice not only motivates them but also instills a sense of accomplishment as they witness their savings grow towards their desired outcomes.

Ultimately, a budget fosters a positive money mindset from a young age. When teenagers actively participate in budgeting, they learn the value of money and the importance of making informed financial choices for themselves. This proactive approach helps them build confidence in their financial abilities and encourages them to be more mindful of their spending habits. By instilling these principles early on, parents can empower their teens to navigate their financial futures with assurance and clarity.

How to Create Your First Budget

Creating your first budget is an essential skill that every teenager should learn. It sets the foundation for a lifetime of financial responsibility and helps young adults understand the value of money. Start by gathering all your income sources, whether it's from a part-time job, allowance, or gifts. Knowing how much money you have will guide your budgeting decisions and help you allocate funds appropriately.

Next, identify your expenses. List both fixed costs, such as subscriptions and savings, and variable costs, like entertainment and dining out which also includes coffees and snacks which can add up. This step allows you to see where your money goes each month. Understanding your spending habits is crucial for making informed decisions and finding areas where you can cut back if necessary.

Once you have a clear picture of your income and expenses, it's time to set financial goals. Whether it's saving for a new gadget, a holiday, or even college, having specific goals gives your budget purpose. Write down these goals and categorize them into short-term and long-term to help you stay motivated and focused on achieving them.

In today's digital age, various money management apps can simplify the budgeting process. Explore options that allow you to track your spending in real-time and set savings goals. Many apps also provide insights into your financial habits, making it easier to adjust your budget as needed. This technology can empower teens to take charge of their finances and build a positive money mindset.

Finally, remember that budgeting is a continuous process. As you grow and your financial situation changes, revisit and adjust your budget regularly. This is important. Embrace the learning journey that comes with managing your money. By starting to budget now, you're laying the groundwork for a secure financial future and developing responsible habits that will serve you well into adulthood.

Tracking Income and Expenses

Tracking income and expenses is a fundamental skill for teenagers embarking on their financial journey. By understanding how to monitor what they earn and spend, young adults can gain valuable insights into their own financial habits. This process not only helps in creating a budget but also fosters a sense of responsibility and self-awareness regarding money management. Parents can play a crucial role in guiding their teens through this essential practice.

Setting up a system for tracking income and expenses can be simple yet effective. Teens can start by keeping a journal or using a spreadsheet to log every source of income, whether it's an allowance, a part time job, or gifts. Likewise, recording expenses, from daily snacks to larger purchases, allows them to see where their money goes. This exercise builds discipline and encourages thoughtful spending, which are key components of financial literacy.

In today's digital age, money management apps provide an excellent resource for tracking finances. These applications can simplify the process, offering features such as automatic expense categorization and budgeting tools. By leveraging technology, teenagers can develop a better understanding of their financial situation while also making tracking more engaging. Parents should encourage their teens to explore these tools to find what works best for them.

Setting financial goals is another vital aspect of managing income and expenses. Encouraging teens to establish both short and long-term goals can motivate them to save and spend wisely. Whether aiming to buy a new gadget or save for a trip, having clear objectives makes it easier to prioritize spending. Parents can assist in this process by discussing the importance of goals and helping their teens break them down into manageable steps.

Ultimately, building a positive money mindset from a young age will serve teenagers well throughout their lives. By actively tracking income and expenses, they cultivate habits that lead to financial stability and success. Parents who engage in these discussions and practices with their teens not only strengthen their relationship, encouraging clear and honest communication, but also empower their children to become financially savvy adults. Emphasizing the importance of money management early on sets the foundation for a secure financial future.

Adjusting Your Budget Over Time

Adjusting your budget over time is crucial for achieving financial stability and success. As teenagers grow and their circumstances change, their budgeting needs will evolve as well. Whether it's a new job, changes in school expenses, or shifts in personal interests, staying adaptable with your finances is vital. This adaptability not only helps in managing current expenses but also prepares young adults for future financial responsibilities.

To begin with, regularly reviewing your budget is essential. Set aside time each month to evaluate your spending and saving habits. This practice allows both parents and teens to identify areas where adjustments can be made, establishing a proactive rather than a reactive approach. Perhaps certain expenses are higher than anticipated, or maybe some income sources have increased. Recognizing these changes will enable you to make informed decisions about where to cut back or invest more.

Another important aspect of adjusting your budget is setting realistic financial goals. Teens should be encouraged to think about what they want to achieve in the short and long term. Whether it's saving for a car, a holiday, or even college funds, these goals can provide motivation to stick to a budget. Parents can play a supportive role by helping their teens outline these goals and incorporate them into their financial plans.

Utilizing technology with the use of money management apps can also aid in adjusting budgets more effectively. These tools offer insights into spending patterns and can help track expenses in real-time. By teaching teens how to use these apps, parents can instill valuable skills that will benefit them throughout their lives. The convenience and accessibility of technology makes it easier to stay on top of financial changes and make necessary adjustments.

Finally, fostering a positive money mindset is key when it comes to financial literacy. Encouraging teens to view budgeting as an empowering activity rather than a restrictive one can lead to a better attitude towards healthier financial habits. Open conversations about money, its value and the importance of making informed decisions will help build a strong foundation for their future.

With the right tools and mindset, adjusting a budget over time can become a rewarding part of financial management for both parents and teens.

Chapter 3: Navigating Money Management Apps for Teens

Overview of Popular Financial Apps

In today's digital age, financial apps have become essential tools for managing money effectively. These applications offer a range of features that help both parents and teenagers budget their finances, track spending, and set financial goals. From tracking daily expenses to saving for future aspirations, these apps simplify the often daunting task of money management. Teens, in particular, can benefit from using these tools to develop healthy financial habits early on, ensuring they are well-prepared for financial independence.

One of the most popular financial apps among young adults is Mint, which provides a comprehensive overview of personal finances. Mint allows users to connect their bank accounts, credit cards, and bills, giving them an accurate picture of their financial situation. The app categorizes expenses, highlights spending trends, and even sends alerts for unusual transactions. Parents can encourage their teens to use Mint to understand where their money goes, fostering a sense of responsibility and awareness about financial choices.

Another noteworthy app is YNAB (You Need A Budget), which focuses on helping users allocate every dollar effectively. YNAB teaches budgeting principles that emphasize proactive financial management rather than reactive habits. This app is especially beneficial for teenagers who are just starting to earn and spend money. By learning to budget their income, teens can cultivate a positive money mindset, setting them up for long-term financial success.

For those looking to save, the app Acorns offers a unique approach to investing. Acorns rounds up everyday purchases to the nearest dollar and invests the spare change into diversified portfolios. This method encourages teens to invest without feeling the pinch of significant contributions. Such an app not only helps in building savings but also instils the importance of investing from a young age, making it an ideal choice for parents who want to teach their children about wealth accumulation.

Lastly, Goalsetter is an education focused financial literacy platform and banking app designed for children and families. As of 2026, the company has announced it is transitioning away from the consumer app to focus primarily on its financial education programs for schools, workplaces and financial institutions. It enables teens and parents to create savings goals for various purposes, like college tuition or a new gadget. By tracking these goals visually, users can stay motivated and celebrate their progress. This app reinforces the idea that setting financial goals is crucial in managing money wisely, helping teens learn the value of planning and perseverance in achieving their aspirations.

Features to Look for in Money Management Apps

When searching for a money management app, it is essential to consider user-friendliness. An intuitive interface allows both parents and teenagers to navigate the app with ease, ensuring that users can quickly access the features they need. A well-designed app should provide clear instructions and support to help young adults manage their nances without feeling overwhelmed. This is particularly important for teenagers who may be using these tools for the first time, making it crucial that the learning curve is reasonable.

Another significant feature to look for is the ability to set and track financial goals. Many teenagers may not have experience with financial planning, so an app that allows them to set specific, achievable goals can be incredibly beneficial. Whether it's saving for a new gadget or understanding how to manage monthly expenses, having a structured way to track these objectives can instill a sense of responsibility and motivation. Parents can also engage with their teens by discussing these goals, reinforcing the importance of financial literacy and accountability.

Security features should also be a top priority when selecting a money management app. Given the sensitivity of financial information, it is vital to choose an app that employs robust security measures to protect user's data. This includes secure login processes, data encryption, and options for two-factor authentication. Parents should ensure that the app they recommend to their teens prioritizes these security features to foster a safe environment for financial management.

Additionally, integration with bank accounts and other financial tools can significantly enhance the app's functionality. This feature allows users to view their entire financial picture in one place, making it easier to track spending, income, and savings. By connecting to their bank accounts, teenagers can gain valuable insights into their spending habits and learn how to budget effectively. This holistic view can help them develop good financial habits early on.

Finally, the app should offer educational resources that promote financial literacy. Many apps provide articles, videos, or interactive tools that can teach users about budgeting, saving, and investing. Access to these resources can also empower teenagers to make informed financial decisions and develop a positive money mindset from a young age as well. By choosing an app that prioritizes education, parents can ensure their teens are not just managing money but also learning essential life skills that will benefit them in the long run.

How to Use Apps Effectively for Budgeting

In today's digital age, budgeting apps offer an effective way for teenagers and their parents to manage finances together. These applications can simplify the budgeting process by allowing users to track their income, expenses, and savings goals in real-time. By engaging with these tools, teenagers can develop essential money management skills that will serve them well into adulthood. Parents can also play a vital role by guiding their teens in selecting the right app that aligns with their financial goals and lifestyle aspirations.

When choosing a budgeting app, it's important to consider the features that best suit your family's needs. Some apps focus on expense tracking, while others may offer savings goal-setting or investment tracking. Look for apps that provide a user-friendly interface, as teenagers are more likely to engage with a tool that is easy to navigate. Additionally, many apps allow for customized categories, enabling users to tailor their budgets to reflect their personal spending habits and priorities.

Setting financial goals is a crucial aspect of effective budgeting. Encourage teenagers to set short-term and long-term goals, whether it's saving for a new gadget, a holiday, or future education. By using budgeting apps to monitor these goals, teens can experience the satisfaction of seeing their progress visually, which can motivate them to stick to their budget. Parents can assist by discussing these goals regularly and helping teens adjust their budgets as needed to achieve them.

Building a positive money mindset from a young age is essential for financial success. Budgeting apps can facilitate this by offering educational resources and tips that promote healthy financial habits. Parents should encourage their teens to explore these resources within the apps, fostering a sense of responsibility and independence in managing their money. This proactive approach not only empowers teens but also strengthens the parent-teen relationship as they work together towards financial literacy.

Ultimately, the effective use of budgeting apps can pave the way for a brighter financial future for teenagers. By actively engaging with these tools, they learn the importance of budgeting, saving, and setting financial goals. With the right guidance and support from parents, teens can harness the power of technology to cultivate lasting money management skills. This journey not only prepares them for adult financial responsibilities but also instills confidence in their ability to make informed financial decisions.

Security and Privacy Considerations

In today's digital age, security and privacy are paramount, particularly when it comes to financial matters. For teenagers managing their money through various apps, understanding how to protect personal information is crucial. Parents should engage in conversations with their teens about the importance of safeguarding their financial data and the potential risks associated with sharing information online. By fostering an environment of open communication, families can work together to navigate the complexities of financial security.

Budgeting apps and money management tools can offer invaluable assistance to young adults, but they also come with responsibilities. Teens should learn to identify secure apps that prioritize user data protection. Parents can help by reviewing app permissions together, ensuring that their children understand what data is being collected and how it is used. This proactive approach not only enhances security but also encourages a sense of responsibility in managing personal finances.

Setting financial goals is an essential part of money management, and privacy considerations play a significant role in this process. When creating budgets or tracking expenses, teens should be mindful of how their financial objectives may be shared or stored within various platforms. Parents can guide their teens in establishing clear boundaries around their financial information, promoting a culture of privacy that reinforces the importance of keeping sensitive data confidential.

Moreover, cultivating a positive money mindset involves recognizing the value of financial literacy, which includes understanding the implications of security and privacy. Teens should be encouraged to ask questions about their financial tools and seek clarification on how to protect themselves online. This not only builds confidence in their financial abilities but also instills a sense of vigilance regarding their own personal information.

Ultimately, the journey towards financial independence for teenagers is intertwined with the principles of security and privacy. By educating themselves and their children about these crucial aspects, parents can empower their teens to make informed decisions. Together, they can establish a foundation that prioritizes both sound financial practices and the protection of personal information, ensuring a more secure financial future for the younger generation.

Chapter 4: The Importance of Setting Financial Goals

Understanding Short-Term vs Long-Term Goals

Understanding the differences between short-term and long-term financial goals is crucial for young adults as they begin their financial journeys. Short-term goals are typically those that can be achieved within a year, such as saving for a new phone or a weekend getaway. These goals are generally more tangible and can provide immediate satisfaction once attained. By focusing on these smaller objectives, teenagers can build confidence in their money management skills while learning the importance of saving and budgeting.

On the other hand, long-term goals often span several years and require a more strategic approach. Examples include saving for college tuition, buying a car, or even planning for retirement. These goals can seem daunting at first, but breaking them down into smaller, actionable steps can make them more achievable. Parents can play a vital role in guiding their teens through this process, helping them to envision their future and understand the importance of persistence and patience.

The interplay between short-term and long-term goals is essential for effective financial planning. Short term goals can serve as stepping stones towards long-term aspirations, providing motivation and a sense of accomplishment along the way. When young people set and achieve short-term goals, they not only develop their financial skills but also learn to appreciate the value of delayed gratification and patience, which is crucial for reaching their long-term objectives.

Money management apps can be beneficial tools in this regard, as they often allow users to set both types of goals and track their progress. Many apps provide features that help teenagers budget, save and invest, making the journey towards financial literacy more interactive and engaging. Parents should encourage their teens to explore these digital resources, as they can simplify the process of managing finances and setting realistic goals.

Ultimately, instilling the habit of setting and pursuing both short-term and long-term financial goals can lay the groundwork for a positive money mindset. By understanding the significance of these goals, teenagers can cultivate good financial habits that will serve them well into adulthood. Encouraging open conversations about money management and goal setting within families can empower young adults to take control of their financial futures with confidence and clarity.

How to Set Realistic and Achievable Goals

Setting realistic and achievable goals is vital for teenagers as they embark on their financial journeys. It is essential to understand that goals should be specific, measurable, achievable, relevant, and time-bound often referred to as the SMART criteria. This framework helps young adults clarify their financial aspirations and provides a structured approach to reaching them. Parents can assist by encouraging their teens to articulate what they truly want to achieve financially, whether it's saving for a new gadget or planning for future education costs.

One practical way to start is by breaking down larger goals into smaller, manageable steps. For example, if the goal is to save a certain amount of money, teens can create a savings plan that outlines how much they need to save weekly or monthly. This not only makes the goal seem less daunting but also instills a sense of accomplishment as they track their progress. Parents can act as accountability partners, helping their children stay on track and celebrate milestones along the way.

Incorporating modern technology can also enhance the goal-setting process. There are numerous money management apps that can assist teenagers in budgeting and monitoring their savings. These apps often come with features that allow users to set up financial goals, track spending, and receive reminders about saving. By leveraging these tools, teens can gain a clearer understanding of their financial habits and make adjustments as necessary, fostering a proactive approach to money management.

Moreover, it's important to instill a positive money mindset from a young age. Encouraging teens to view their financial goals as opportunities for growth rather than obstacles can significantly affect their motivation. Teaching them the value of patience and perseverance in achieving their goals can help build resilience. When teenagers understand that financial success is a journey, they are more likely to remain committed to their objectives, even when faced with challenges.

Lastly, parents should lead by example. Sharing personal experiences related to goal setting, financial management as well as their own past challenges can provide valuable lessons for teens. Discussing financial successes and failures openly can demystify money management and encourage honest, healthy dialogue within the family. By working together to set and achieve realistic financial goals, parents and teens can strengthen their relationship while fostering essential life skills that will benefit them in the future.

The Role of Saving and Achieving Goals

Saving money is a fundamental skill that plays a crucial role in achieving personal financial goals. For teenagers, understanding the importance of saving can lead to better money management habits in adulthood. By setting aside a portion of their allowance or earnings, young adults can learn how to budget effectively and make informed financial decisions. This practice not only prepares them for future expenses but also teaches them the value of delayed gratification, which is essential in a world filled with instant temptations.

Incorporating saving into a teenager's financial routine helps them develop a positive money mindset from a young age. By regularly saving towards a specific goal, teens can experience the satisfaction of achieving something they have worked hard for. This sense of accomplishment reinforces the idea that saving is not just about denying oneself enjoyment, but rather about prioritizing and planning for future goals. It instills a sense of control over their finances, which is empowering as they transition into adulthood.

Parents can play an active role in teaching their teens about saving by encouraging them to set realistic financial goals. Whether it's saving for a new bike or contributing to a future college fund, having a clear target can motivate teenagers to save consistently. Parents can also introduce money management apps that help track savings progress, making the process engaging and educational. These tools allow teens to visualize their savings and understand how small contributions can add up over time, making the concept of saving more tangible.

Moreover, creating a savings plan together can strengthen the parent-teen relationship. By discussing financial goals openly, parents can share their own experiences and lessons learned about money management. This dialogue not only provides valuable insights but also fosters an environment where financial literacy is taken seriously. By making saving a family affair, parents can inspire their teens to develop lifelong habits that will benefit them financially with their own families in the future.

Ultimately, the role of saving and achieving goals cannot be expressed enough. It equips teenagers with the skills they need to navigate financial challenges and seize opportunities as they arise. By understanding the significance of saving, young adults can approach their future with confidence, knowing they have the means to achieve their aspirations. This foundational knowledge is essential in fostering a generation that values financial literacy and responsibly manages their money.

Celebrating Milestones

Celebrating milestones is an essential part of developing a positive money mindset. For teenagers, reaching financial goals, no matter how small, can significantly boost their confidence and motivation. When a teen saves for something new or manages to stick to a budget for a month, it's important for parents to acknowledge these achievements. Celebrations can take many forms, from a special dinner out to a small gift, reinforcing the idea that hard work and smart financial decisions are worthy of recognition.

Moreover, recognizing milestones encourages teenagers to set new financial goals. It cultivates a habit of evaluating their progress and planning for future aspirations. This practice not only empowers them to take charge of their nances but also instills an understanding that financial literacy isn't just about saving money, it's about making informed choices that lead to personal fulfillment. By celebrating each accomplishment, parents can help their teens appreciate the journey of financial growth.

In addition, using money management apps can serve as a fun and interactive way to track these milestones. Many apps provide visual representations of progress, such as graphs and charts, which make the learning process engaging for young adults. Parents can encourage their teens to explore different features of these apps that allow them to set, track, and celebrate their financial goals. This not only enhances their understanding of money management but also integrates technology into their financial education.

Setting financial goals is crucial, but celebrating their achievement is just as vital. Parents should involve their teens in discussions about their goals and the steps needed to reach them. This open dialogue fosters a sense of responsibility and ownership over their financial journey. When goals are met, whether it's saving a certain amount or budgeting successfully, a celebration acts as a powerful motivator for teens to continue striving for excellence.

Ultimately, celebrating milestones creates a positive feedback loop that reinforces good financial habits.
As teenagers learn to value their achievements, they develop a constructive relationship with money. Parents play a key role in this process by providing encouragement and recognition. By making celebrations a regular practice, families can create an environment where financial literacy thrives, setting the stage for a bright financial future for teenagers.

Chapter 5: Building a Positive Money Mindset

Understanding Your Attitude Towards Money

Understanding your attitude towards money is crucial for developing healthy financial habits. Many people carry beliefs about money that are shaped by their upbringing, experiences, and societal influences. For teenagers, this understanding is particularly important as they begin to make their own financial decisions. Parents play a key role in guiding their children to recognize and reflect on their money attitudes, setting the foundation for responsible financial behavior in adulthood.

A positive money mindset can lead to better budgeting practices and more effective money management. Teens must learn that money is a tool that can help them achieve their goals, rather than something to be feared or mismanaged. Encouraging discussions about money within the family can demystify finances and promote a healthier relationship with spending and saving. This dialogue can also help teenagers identify any negative beliefs they might have about money and work towards shifting those perspectives.

In today's digital age, understanding money management apps is essential for young adults. These tools can assist teens in tracking their spending, setting budgets, and planning for future expenses. By familiarizing themselves with these resources, teens can develop a more hands-on approach to their finances. Parents should encourage their children to explore various apps and find ones that resonate with their financial goals, enhancing their experience with budgeting.

Setting financial goals is an integral part of cultivating a positive attitude towards money. When teens establish clear, achievable objectives, they are more likely to stay motivated and engaged in their financial journey. Parents can support their children by helping them to define short-term and long-term goals, whether it's saving for a new gadget or planning for college. This practice not only builds financial literacy but also instills a sense of responsibility and ownership over their financial decisions.

Ultimately, understanding and improving one's attitude towards money is a lifelong journey. By fostering an environment where financial discussions are encouraged, teens can develop a healthy relationship with money from a young age. This positive foundation will serve them well as they navigate the complexities of personal nance in adulthood. Parents and teens alike should work together to ensure that financial literacy becomes an integral part of their lives, paving the way for a secure financial future.

Overcoming Common Financial Fears

Financial fears can often feel overwhelming, especially for teenagers who are just beginning to navigate the world of money. These fears may stem from a lack of understanding about budgeting, saving, and managing expenses. Parents play a crucial role in helping their teens overcome these anxieties by providing guidance and support. By fostering open, honest, conversations about finances, families can create a safe space for discussing concerns and building confidence in financial decision-making.

One common fear among teenagers is the worry of not having enough money to meet their needs or wants. This fear can lead to anxiety about budgeting and saving. Parents can help by teaching their teens the basics of budgeting, which involves tracking income and expenses. By using simple budgeting apps, young adults can learn to manage their finances effectively and gain a sense of control over their money, alleviating some of their fears.

Setting financial goals is another essential aspect of overcoming financial fears. Teens may feel daunted by the prospect of saving for larger purchases or future needs. Parents can encourage their children to set realistic and achievable financial goals. By breaking down these goals into smaller, manageable steps, teens can experience a sense of accomplishment as they progress, which can further reduce their fears about money.

Building a positive money mindset from a young age is crucial in overcoming financial anxieties. Parents can model healthy financial behaviors and attitudes, demonstrating that money management is not something to fear but rather an empowering skill. Encouraging discussions about financial successes and lessons learned can help teens develop a more positive outlook on money, transforming their fears into motivation for responsible financial habits.

In conclusion, addressing and overcoming common financial fears is an essential part of teaching financial literacy to teenagers. By engaging in open dialogue, teaching budgeting skills, setting goals, and fostering a positive mindset, parents and teens can work together to ensure a brighter financial future. This collaborative effort not only diminishes fear but also equips young adults with the tools they need to navigate their financial journeys confidently.

Developing Healthy Financial Habits

Developing healthy financial habits is essential for teenagers as they embark on their journey towards financial independence. Parents play a crucial role in guiding their teens through the basics of budgeting, helping them understand the importance of tracking their income and expenses. By establishing a budget, young adults can learn to allocate their resources wisely, ensuring that they make informed decisions about their spending and saving habits. This foundational skill sets the stage for a more secure financial future.

In today's digital age, utilizing money management apps can significantly enhance a teenager's ability to manage their finances effectively. These tools offer a user-friendly interface that makes tracking expenses and setting financial goals straightforward and engaging. By encouraging teenagers to explore various apps, parents can help them find one that suits their needs and preferences. This not only fosters independence but also provides a sense of control over their financial situation.

Setting financial goals is another vital aspect of developing healthy financial habits. Teens should learn to set short-term and long-term goals that are specific, measurable, achievable, relevant, and time-bound (SMART). By working towards these goals, teenagers can cultivate a sense of accomplishment and motivation, which reinforces positive money management behaviors. Parents can support this process by discussing their own financial goals and sharing experiences to illustrate the importance of planning for the future.

Building a positive money mindset from a young age is crucial for instilling lifelong financial literacy. Encouraging open discussions about money, saving, and spending can help demystify financial concepts and reduce anxiety around these topics. Parents should model healthy financial behaviors, demonstrating how to handle money responsibly. By fostering an environment where financial conversations are welcomed, teenagers will be more likely to adopt a proactive approach to their finances, leading to better outcomes in adulthood.

Ultimately, developing healthy financial habits is a journey that requires ongoing support and encouragement from parents. By focusing on budgeting basics, exploring money management apps, setting financial goals, and nurturing a positive money mindset, parents can equip their teenagers with the tools they need to navigate their financial futures successfully. This collaborative effort not only strengthens the parent-teen relationship but also lays a solid foundation for a lifetime of financial wellbeing.

The Power of Gratitude and Generosity

Gratitude and generosity serve as powerful tools in shaping a positive financial mindset for both teenagers and their parents. When young adults learn to appreciate what they have, they cultivate a sense of contentment that can reduce the desire for unnecessary spending. This appreciation fosters resilience against consumerism, enabling them to make wiser financial decisions. By understanding the value of gratitude, teens can better navigate their financial journeys with a sense of purpose and clarity.

Incorporating acts of generosity into their lives can also have profound effects on young adult's financial perspectives. When teenagers give back, whether through volunteering, sharing resources, or helping others in need, they develop empathy and a broader understanding of financial realities. This practice not only builds character but also reinforces the idea that financial success is not solely about personal gain. By seeing the impact of their generosity, teens can feel a deeper connection to their community and an enhanced sense of responsibility.

Moreover, parents play a crucial role in modeling gratitude and generosity. When families engage in discussions about money management that include the value of giving, it creates a supportive environment for learning. Parents can encourage their teens to set financial goals that reflect both personal aspirations and a commitment to helping others. This balance of self-care and altruism can lead to a more rounded approach to financial literacy, where money is viewed as a tool for positive change.

Utilizing money management apps can further support the practice of gratitude and generosity among teenagers. Many of these apps feature budgeting tools that allow young adults to track their expenses and savings while setting aside funds for charitable giving. By visually seeing their financial progress and how they allocate resources, teens can cultivate a mindful attitude towards spending and sharing. This technological support reinforces the lessons of gratitude and generosity in a modern context, making financial literacy more accessible.

Ultimately, the power of gratitude and generosity can transform the way teenagers view money and its role in their lives. By embracing these principles, they can develop a positive money mindset that not only benefits their financial health but also enriches their relationships and community ties. As parents and teens work together to integrate these values, they can create a financial future that is not only prosperous but also compassionate, fostering a generation that values both personal and collective well-being.

Chapter 6: Involving Parents in Financial Learning

The Role of Parents in Financial Education

Parents play a crucial role in shaping their children's financial literacy and understanding of money management. By fostering an environment where discussions about money are open and encouraged, parents can help their teens develop essential budgeting skills. This foundational knowledge is vital as young adults prepare to navigate their financial lives independently. Parents who actively engage in these discussions can demystify financial concepts and serve as valuable resources for their children.

One of the most effective ways parents can teach financial education is through practical examples. When parents create and adhere to a family budget, they model sound financial behaviors. Teens learn best by observing, so seeing their parents manage expenses, save for goals, and prioritize needs over wants provides a real-life context for these lessons. Additionally, involving teens in family financial decisions, such as planning for holidays or larger purchases, can give them hands-on experience in budgeting.

Setting financial goals is another area where parental guidance is essential. Parents should encourage their teens to set both short-term and long-term financial goals. This can include saving for a new gadget or planning for future education expenses. By helping their children establish clear, achievable goals, parents instill a sense of purpose in their financial dealings, making money management more meaningful and motivating for teens.

In today's digital age, understanding money management apps is increasingly important. Parents can assist their teens in exploring various financial apps that promote budgeting, saving, and tracking expenses. By guiding them through the features of these tools, parents can help teens harness technology to enhance their financial literacy. This partnership in exploring apps not only educates teens but also strengthens the parent-child relationship by fostering teamwork in managing finances.

Ultimately, building a positive money mindset from a young age is vital for financial success. Parents must emphasize the importance of resilience, patience, and a growth mindset when it comes to money. By discussing both the challenges and successes of financial management openly, parents can help their teens navigate setbacks and celebrate achievements, ensuring they approach their financial futures with confidence and optimism.

Open Conversations About Money

Open conversations about money are essential for fostering a healthy financial mindset in teenagers. Parents play a crucial role in guiding their children through the complexities of financial literacy. By initiating discussions around budgeting, saving, and spending, families can create an environment where young adults feel comfortable exploring their financial aspirations and challenges. Such openness not only demystifies money management but also encourages responsible decision-making from an early age.

Budgeting basics should be a key topic in these discussions. Teaching teenagers how to create a budget helps them understand the value of money and the importance of setting financial priorities. Parents can involve their teens in real-life budgeting scenarios, such as planning for a family outing or saving for a special purchase. This hands-on experience reinforces the concepts of income, expenses, and savings, making the learning process both practical and engaging.

Understanding money management apps is another vital aspect of modern financial literacy. With technology at their fingertips, teenagers can easily access tools that simplify budgeting and tracking expenses. Parents should encourage their teens to explore these apps together, discussing their features and benefits. This collaborative approach not only familiarizes teenagers with useful resources but also empowers them to take charge of their financial habits in a digital age.

Setting financial goals is a powerful way for teenagers to learn about the significance of planning for the future. Parents can help their teens identify short-term and long-term goals, such as saving for a new gadget or planning for college. By regularly reviewing and adjusting these goals, families can instill a sense of accountability and motivation in young adults. This practice fosters a proactive attitude towards money management, making it easier for them to navigate financial challenges as they arise.

Finally, building a positive money mindset from a young age is crucial for lifelong financial success. Parents should encourage their teens to adopt a healthy relationship with money, focusing on abundance rather than scarcity. Discussions about financial successes and setbacks can help normalize these experiences, reinforcing the idea that learning from mistakes is part of the journey. By promoting a positive outlook on finances, parents can equip their teenagers with the confidence to face their financial futures with resilience and optimism.

Family Activities to Promote Financial Literacy

Engaging in family activities that promote financial literacy can significantly benefit both parents and teenagers. One effective way to start is by creating a family budget together. This activity allows everyone to contribute their thoughts on income and expenses, fostering a sense of responsibility and teamwork. By discussing priorities and making decisions as a family, teenagers learn the basic principles of budgeting while feeling valued in the process.

Another insightful activity is to set financial goals as a family unit. This could include saving for a family holiday, a new car, or even a charity donation. By working towards a common aim, teenagers can grasp the concept of setting realistic financial goals and the importance of saving. This collective effort not only builds collaboration but also strengthens family bonds as everyone contributes towards achieving the target.

Incorporating technology can also enhance financial literacy. Parents can introduce their teens to various money management apps that track spending and budgeting. By exploring these tools together, families can discuss their features and how they can aid in effective money management. This hands-on experience with technology can empower teenagers to take control of their finances while also making the learning process enjoyable.

Family discussions about money are crucial and can be initiated during regular family meetings. These conversations can cover topics such as the importance of saving, investing, and understanding debt. Encouraging open dialogue about finances helps demystify money matters for teenagers. They will feel more confident asking questions and expressing their thoughts, leading to a more profound understanding of financial concepts.

Lastly, cultivating a positive money mindset from a young age is essential. Families can engage in activities that promote gratitude and appreciation for money, such as discussing the value of experiences over material possessions. By instilling a healthy attitude towards finances, parents can help their teens develop a balanced outlook on money, which will serve them well into adulthood. This encouraging environment nurtures financial literacy and prepares young adults for a successful future.

Encouraging Joint Goal Setting

Setting financial goals together can be a transformative experience for both parents and teenagers. It promotes open communication about money, allowing families to discuss their financial values and aspirations. By engaging in joint goal setting, parents can guide their teens in understanding the importance of budgeting and saving, helping them to develop a more responsible attitude towards money management from an early age.

When teens are involved in creating their financial goals, they are more likely to feel empowered and accountable for their decisions. Parents can encourage this process by facilitating discussions around short-term and long-term objectives, such as saving for a new gadget or planning for college tuition. By breaking down these goals into manageable steps, families can create a roadmap that not only fosters financial literacy but also strengthens their bond as they work towards shared aspirations.

Utilizing money management apps can enhance the joint goal setting experience. These tools provide a platform for tracking progress, budgeting, and managing expenses together. Parents can introduce their teens to various apps that offer features tailored for young adults, making the process of monitoring their financial goals engaging and interactive. This tech-savvy approach can help demystify money management and instill a sense of responsibility in teenagers.

Moreover, setting financial goals as a family encourages a positive money mindset. When parents model healthy financial behaviors and involve their teens in discussions about money, it demystifies what can often be a daunting subject. By celebrating small successes along the way, families can create an environment where financial achievements are recognized and valued, reinforcing the importance of persistence and discipline in achieving one's goals.

In conclusion, encouraging joint goal setting lays the foundation for a future of financial literacy and responsible money management. Parents and teens who collaborate on financial objectives not only work towards their individual aspirations but also foster a deeper understanding of the value of money. This collaborative approach not only prepares teenagers for their financial futures but also nurtures their relationship with money, making it a lifelong skill that can lead to financial independence and security.

Chapter 7: Real-Life Applications of Financial Literacy

Case Studies of Successful Young Savers

In today's world, the importance of financial literacy cannot be overstated, especially for young people. Case studies of successful young savers provide inspiring examples of how teenagers can take charge of their financial futures. These individuals demonstrate that with the right knowledge, tools, and mindset, anyone can achieve their financial goals, regardless of their starting point. Their experiences serve as powerful reminders that it's never too early to start on the path to financial independence.

One such case is that of my oldest daughter Rachael, at 17, began saving for her first car at the age of 15. By using a budgeting app, she tracked her expenses and identified areas where she could cut back. This discipline allowed her to save a significant portion of her allowance and part-time job earnings. Rachael's story illustrates the effectiveness of modern money management apps in helping young people organize their nances and work towards their goals.

Another inspiring example is my nephew Brandon, who, at 16, set a financial goal to save for college. He researched scholarships and part-time jobs, understanding the importance of planning ahead. By actively seeking opportunities and budgeting his income, Brandon not only saved money but also gained valuable life skills. His proactive approach highlights the importance of setting financial goals and the impact this can have on a young person's life.

Furthermore, the journey of my youngest daughter Sarah, who started a small bakery business at 15, showcases the entrepreneurial spirit of today's youth. Through her venture, she learned about budgeting, marketing, and customer service. Sarah's experience underscores the importance of building a positive money mindset from a young age, as her business not only provided her with an income but also instilled confidence and financial acumen that will benefit her in the future.

These case studies collectively illustrate that successful young savers are not just lucky, they are informed and proactive. They embrace financial literacy as a lifelong journey, using available resources and setting clear goals. By sharing these stories, we hope to inspire teenagers and their parents to engage in financial discussions and encourage the development of smart money habits that will last a lifetime.

Practical Exercises for Parents and Teens

Practical exercises are essential for parents and teens to engage actively in financial literacy. One effective exercise is creating a shared budgeting worksheet. Parents can sit down with their teenagers to list income sources, such as allowances or part-time jobs, and outline their monthly expenses. This collaborative effort not only teaches budgeting basics but also fosters communication about money, ensuring that both parties understand the importance of tracking spending.

Another insightful exercise involves setting financial goals together. Parents and teens can brainstorm short-term and long-term financial aspirations, such as saving for a new gadget or a car. By discussing these goals, they can learn the significance of prioritizing their spending and develop strategies to achieve these objectives. This practice reinforces the idea that financial planning is a continuous process that requires dedication and teamwork.

Incorporating technology into financial education can also be beneficial. Parents can introduce their teens to money management apps that help track expenses and savings. An exercise could be to set a challenge where teens use an app for a month to monitor their spending habits. This hands-on experience will not only familiarize them with modern financial tools but also instill a sense of responsibility and awareness about their financial choices.

Building a positive money mindset is crucial for young adults. Parents can encourage their teens to reflect on their attitudes towards money through journaling or discussions. They can explore questions like, "What does money mean to you?" or "How do you feel when you spend or save?" These reflections can lead to a better understanding of their financial behaviors and help them cultivate a healthier relationship with money from an early age.

Lastly, parents can organize family activities that revolve around financial themes, such as visiting a bank or attending a financial literacy workshop together. Such experiences can make learning about money enjoyable and interactive. By participating in these exercises, both parents and teens will not only improve their financial literacy but also create lasting memories and strengthen their bond as they embark on this essential journey of financial awareness together.

Resources for Continued Learning

In today's fast-paced world, the journey to financial literacy is ongoing, and there are numerous resources available to both parents and teenagers. Websites such as the National Endowment for Financial Education (NEFE) provide a wealth of information tailored specifically for young adults. These platforms offer interactive tools and educational materials that can help teenagers grasp the basics of budgeting, saving, and investing. By exploring these resources together, parents can engage in meaningful discussions about money management with their teens.

Additionally, many local libraries and community centers host workshops focused on financial literacy. These events often include expert speakers who can share valuable insights and strategies for managing money effectively. Parents should encourage their teenagers to participate in these workshops, as they provide a supportive environment for learning and asking questions. Attending such sessions can also help teens connect with peers who are on the same journey towards financial understanding.

Financial management apps have become increasingly popular among young adults, offering a convenient way to track spending, create budgets, and set financial goals. Apps such as Mint or YNAB (You Need A Budget) can simplify money management and provide teenagers with real-time data about their nances. Parents can assist their teens in selecting the right app, ensuring that it aligns with their financial goals. Learning to use these tools effectively can empower young adults to take control of their financial futures.

Setting financial goals is another crucial aspect of financial literacy that should be emphasized. Parents and teens can work together to identify short-term and long-term financial objectives, such as saving for a new phone or planning for college expenses. By establishing clear goals, teenagers learn the importance of budgeting and saving, which are essential skills for adult life. Regularly reviewing and adjusting these goals can help maintain motivation and foster a proactive approach to money management.

Lastly, cultivating a positive money mindset from a young age is vital for future financial success. Encouraging open discussions about money, instilling values of saving and sharing, and celebrating financial achievements can help teenagers develop a healthy relationship with money. Parents play a critical role in modeling these behaviors, demonstrating how to handle financial challenges with resilience and optimism. By embracing these resources and strategies, families can pave the way for a financially literate and con dent generation.

The Journey Ahead: Lifelong Financial Literacy

As we embark on the journey of lifelong financial literacy, it is essential to understand that this path begins in adolescence. For teenagers, grasping the fundamentals of money management can set the stage for a future filled with financial stability. Parents play a crucial role in this process, guiding their teens through the basics of budgeting, saving, and spending wisely. By fostering an environment where financial discussions are encouraged, families can help young adults develop the skills necessary to navigate their financial futures successfully.

Budgeting is one of the first steps in mastering financial literacy. Young adults should learn how to create a budget that reflects their income and expenses, enabling them to manage their money effectively. This skill not only helps in tracking spending but also instills a sense of responsibility. By involving teens in the budgeting process, parents can teach them the importance of distinguishing between needs and wants, ultimately guiding them towards making informed financial decisions.

In today's digital age, money management apps have become indispensable tools for teenagers. These applications can simplify budgeting and tracking expenses, making financial literacy more accessible. By encouraging teens to utilize these apps, parents can help them stay organized and develop good financial habits. Furthermore, familiarizing young adults with technology in this context prepares them for a future where digital finance will play a significant role in their lives.

Setting financial goals is another vital aspect of lifelong financial literacy. Teens should be encouraged to establish both short-term and long-term goals, whether it's saving for a new gadget, a holiday, or future education. Teaching them to set realistic goals helps cultivate discipline and patience, allowing them to see the fruits of their efforts over time. This practice not only motivates young adults but also instills a sense of achievement as they reach their financial milestones.

Finally, building a positive money mindset from a young age is crucial for fostering financial success. Encouraging teens to view money as a tool for achieving their dreams rather than a source of stress can dramatically change their perspective. By promoting discussions around financial positivity and resilience, parents can help their children develop a healthy relationship with money, paving the way for a lifetime of sound financial practices. This journey of financial literacy is not merely about managing money, it's about empowering young adults to make informed decisions that will benefit them throughout their lives.

MONTHLY BUDGET PLANNER

DATE:

INCOME/ALLOWANCE/GIFTS

DATE	DESCRIPTION	AMOUNT
	TOTAL:	

EXPENSES

DATE	DESCRIPTION	AMOUNT
	TOTAL:	

SAVINGS

INCOME - EXPENSES = TOTAL	